I0605237

MISSION: SPACE SCIENCE

THE INNER PLANETS

Sarah Eason

Use Your STEM Skills to Explore Our Nearest Neighbors

Published in 2025 by **Cheriton Children's Books**
1 Bank Drive West, Shrewsbury, Shropshire, SY3 9DJ

First Edition

Author: Sarah Eason
Designers: Paul Myerscough and Steve Mead
Editor: Jennifer Sanderson
Proofreader: Ella Newby
Consultant: David Hawksett, BSc

Picture credits: Cover: Shutterstock/Rdrgraphe (t), Shutterstock/Buradaki (b). Inside: pp4-05: Shutterstock/Christos Georghiou, p6: Shutterstock/Gilmanshin, p7: Shutterstock/Claudio Caridi, p8: Wikimedia Commons/Cristiano Banti, p9: Wikimedia Commons/Galileo Galilei, p10: Shutterstock/Claudio Caridi, p11: NASA/Johns Hopkins University Applied Physics Laboratory/Carnegie Institution of Washington, p12: NASA/Johns Hopkins University Applied Physics Laboratory/Carnegie Institution of Washington, p13: Shutterstock/Designua, p14: Shutterstock/DestinaDesign, p15b: Wikimedia Commons/Shisma, p15t: Wikimedia Commons/Francesco Giovanni Cantagalli, p16: ESA/JAXA, p17: ESA/JAXA, p18: NASA/JPL, p19: NASA/JSC, p20: Shutterstock/Artsiom P, p21: Shutterstock/Dotted Yeti, p22l: NASA, p22r: Shutterstock/Buradaki, p23: Shutterstock/Tom Hirtreiter, p24: Shutterstock/Anna Marin N, p25: Shutterstock/AlexLMX, p26: ESA, p27: CNSA, p28: NASA/JPL-Caltech, p29b: NASA/JPL, p29t: ESA/DLR/FUBerlin/AndreaLuck, p30b: NASA, p30t: NASA/JPL-Caltech/University of Arizona, p31: Shutterstock/Dotted Yeti, p32: Shutterstock/Limbitech, p33: NASA/JPL-Caltech/MSSS, p34: NASA/JSC, p35: NASA/MSFC, p36b: Shutterstock/Frame Stock Footage, p36t: NASA/Crew of STS-132, p37: NASA, p38: NASA/Clouds AO/SEArch, p39: Shutterstock/Stockbym, p40: ESA/ATG Medialab, p41: Wikimedia Commons/COMEX, p42: Wikimedia Commons/Andrzej Mirecki, p43: Shutterstock/Vadim Sadovski, p44: NASA, p45: Shutterstock/Lia Koltyrina.

Printed in China

CONTENTS

Chapter 1

THE SOLAR SYSTEM

Somewhere within the vastness of the universe, hundreds of billions of stars swirl around a central point. It is not easy to find; this galaxy is just one of hundreds of billions like it, strewn throughout the vast universe. On one of the galaxy's arms, about 27,000 light-years from the center, lies a medium-sized star. The star is surrounded by rocky spheres, gaseous balls, icy lumps, and countless fragments of rock. That medium-sized star is the sun.

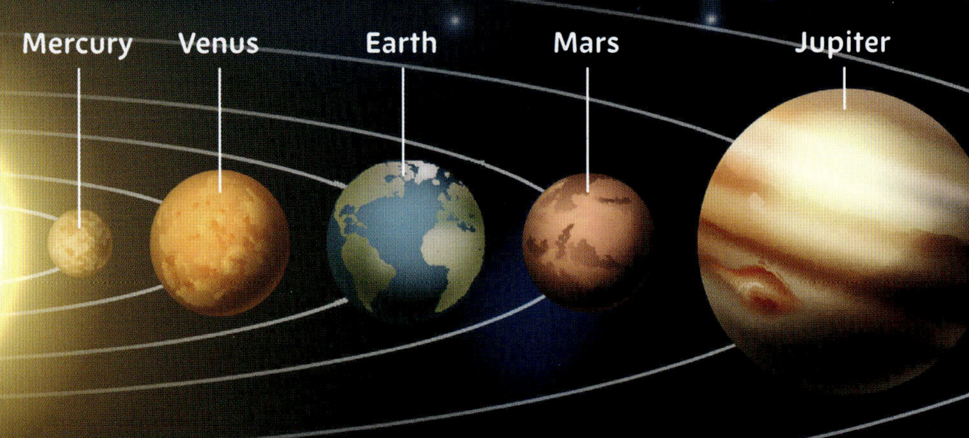

SPACE SCIENCE

In 2006, astronomers changed the definition of a planet. They said that a planet must orbit the sun, and it must be large enough to have a nearly round shape. It must be gravitationally dominant in its orbit. This means that no other objects of a similar size orbit the sun in the same path. The small, rocky dwarf planet Pluto met the first two requirements. It did not, however, meet the third, so it was demoted and considered a dwarf planet.

Our Amazing Star

The four planets closest to the sun—Mercury, Venus, Earth, and Mars—are relatively small and rocky. The other four—Jupiter, Saturn, Uranus, and Neptune—are much larger and mainly made of gas and liquid, with no solid surface.

Our home, Earth, is one of four smaller rocky planets that are in the inner part of the solar system, nearest to our star.

Similar but Different

The inner planets seem similar at first, but they have significant differences. Mercury is tiny and hot, with a heavily cratered surface. Venus is swathed in thick clouds that give it a stifling and toxic atmosphere. Earth has an atmosphere and is mostly covered with huge oceans of liquid water that are teeming with life. Mars has not one but two small, lumpy moons.

YOUR MISSION

In this book we will explore the inner planets in detail, looking at what we know about them and how we learned it. You will also be given thought-provoking space missions to complete that will draw on:

- Your STEM skills: these are science, technology, engineering, and math skills.
- Your social skills: these include identifying skills and strengths in others, team building, persuasive skills, and learning how to work collaboratively.
- Your critical thinking skills: these include being able to evaluate and analyze information, think independently about problems and find solutions, and draw your own conclusions.

All the above skills are vital for successful space exploration—ask any space scientist! So, are you mission-ready? Let's begin the missions and find out.

Ancient Planets

The inner planets can be easily seen with the naked eye, so they have been known since ancient times. Many cultures associated them with gods and goddesses. Even the earliest astronomers realized that planets were different from stars. The stars we see from Earth appear to rotate every 24 hours, but they do not change position relative to each other. The planets, on the other hand, move across the sky over a period of days, and that is how they get their name: *planetes* means "wanderers" in ancient Greek.

Wandering Mercury?

Mercury's pace is anything but wandering. It moves across the sky faster than any other planet, so both the Greeks and the Romans named it after their speedy messenger god. Mercury, the Roman version, was famous for moving quickly between Earth and the heavens.

The planet Mercury gets its name from the fast-moving god Mercury, shown here in this sculpture.

Space Science

The Maya charted the motion of the planet Mercury. Records of their detailed observations include the appearance of Mercury as a morning star in 733 BCE and as an evening star in 727 BCE. The Maya also calculated that Mercury would rise and set in the same place in the sky every 2,200 days.

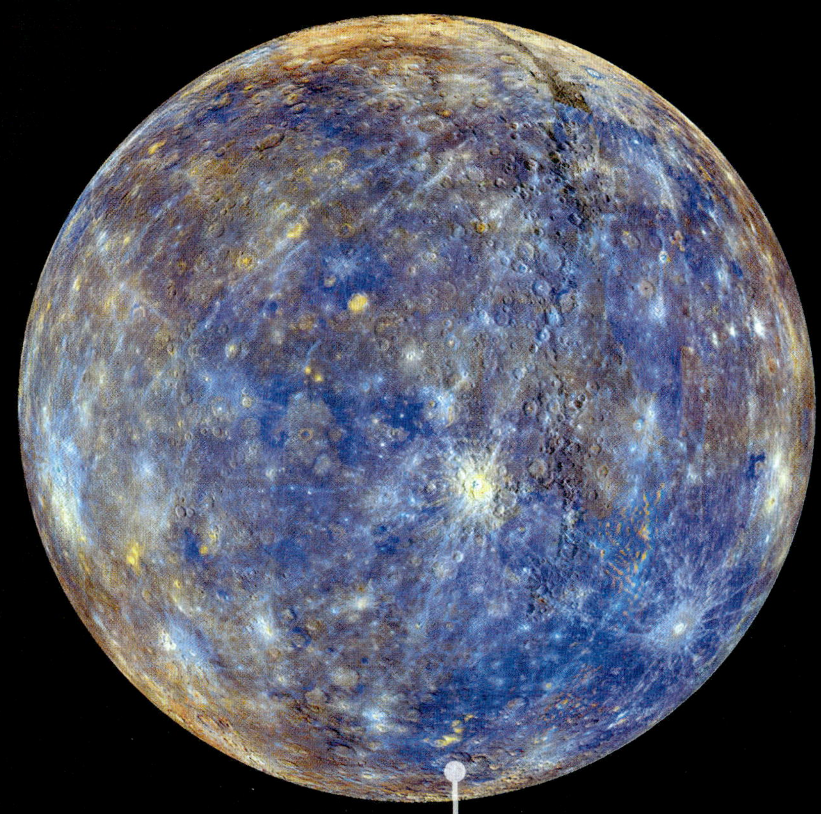

It takes fast-moving Mercury just 88 days to complete one orbit of our star—the sun.

Morning and Evening Star

Like Mercury, Venus is between Earth and the sun, so it was known to several cultures as a morning star and an evening star, with separate names for each. The Babylonians realized these stars were the same planet more than 3,500 years ago. Venus is the closest planet to Earth, which is partly why it appears brighter than the other planets. Many ancient cultures viewed Venus as a female planet. One reason for this was that it was visible for about nine months a year, the same amount of time as a woman is pregnant.

The Planet of War

Mars has a reddish color, even when seen with the naked eye, making it stand out from the other planets. As a result, most ancient cultures associated it with bloody war and death. The Sumerians named it after Nergal, their god of war, and the Greeks and Romans did the same: Ares for the Greeks, and Mars for the Romans.

Mysterious Planets

Although early astronomers were able to track and predict the movement of the planets, there was a lot they did not know. For example, since the planets appear roughly the same size as stars, they did not realize that the stars are so much farther away. They also did not know how the solar system was organized. Many early astronomers put Earth at the center of the solar system (and, indeed, the whole universe).

First Facts

Early astronomers did know that Mercury and Venus were closer to Earth than the sun. The two planets pass between Earth and the sun, and if the alignment is just right, they can be seen as small black circles traveling across the sun. This is called a transit. As a result, most early solar system diagrams had the moon orbiting closest to Earth, followed by Mercury, Venus, the sun, then Mars, Jupiter, and Saturn.

Galileo's beliefs about the solar system, particularly the suggestion that the sun was at its center, caused outrage. The Catholic Church imprisoned the astronomer (shown below, right) because of his scientific theories.

Major Breakthroughs

Once telescopes were invented in the early 1600s, astronomy really took off. The Italian astronomer Galileo Galilei (1564–1642) made a breakthrough when he discovered that Venus has phases. This means that it appears to change shape like the moon does, slowly growing from a crescent shape to a full disc, and then back again. The change in shape is not visible to the naked eye, so Galileo was the first to see the phases. Mercury also has phases, but Galileo's telescope was not powerful enough to view them.

Canals on Mars

Before long, telescopes were powerful enough to show detail on the surface of the planets. Giovanni Schiaparelli (1835–1910), an Italian astronomer, observed linear features on Mars. He called them canali, meaning "channels," but this was mistranslated as "canals." Canals are humanmade, so this led to speculation that there was intelligent life on Mars in the form of Martians!

These are Galileo's sketches of the phases of Venus.

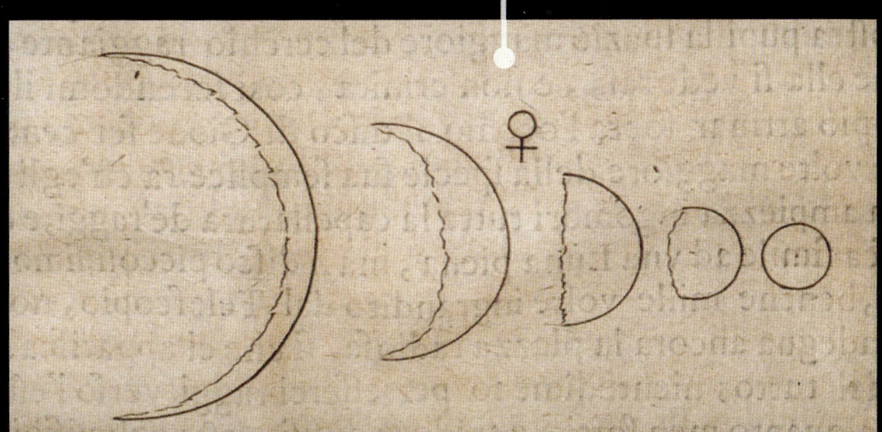

YOUR MISSION

You have been given the task of finding other solar systems in the universe. What key features would you search for, and why? Do you think other solar systems might differ from our own? If so, how?

Chapter 2

DISCOVERING MERCURY

Although Mercury is relatively close to Earth, its position near the sun makes it difficult to view from Earth and difficult for spacecraft to visit. As a result, we know less about it than we know about planets such as Jupiter and Saturn, which are much farther away. In the 1880s, Schiaparelli used a telescope to map part of Mercury's surface, a project that was continued in the 1930s by the Greek-French astronomer, Eugenios Antoniadi (1870–1944).

This color image of Mercury shows features on its surface. Impact marks are shown as light-blue or white lines, with craters as white or light-yellow areas. Medium- and dark-blue areas are thought to be rich in minerals. Tan areas are plains formed by lava.

Radar Lessons

In the 1960s, astronomers started using radar to learn about Mercury. Using radar involves sending microwave radiation toward an object such as a planet and analyzing the signals that bounce back. It is similar to the way a bat uses echolocation to find insects to eat, sending out sounds and listening to how they bounce back. The technique can provide information about the planet's shape and surface features.

Sending in Probes

Only two space probes have visited Mercury so far. The first, Mariner 10, was launched in 1973 to study Venus and Mercury. During a flyby of Venus, it used Venus's gravitational force to bend its path toward Mercury. Mariner 10 was not able to enter orbit around the planet, but it conducted three flybys, looping around the sun between each one. On its third approach, the probe came within 203 miles (327 km) of Mercury's surface, but ran out of fuel before it could loop around the sun again. It is still in orbit somewhere around the sun.

Mission MESSENGER

Much of our data about Mercury comes from the MESSENGER mission that launched in 2004 and finally entered orbit around the planet in 2011. Its goal was to study the planet's composition, geology, and magnetic field. It was a huge success. It mapped Mercury's entire surface in detail, helping us understand the planet's geography as well as making other discoveries. The mission ended in 2015 when MESSENGER crashed into Mercury after it had run out of fuel.

This artist's image shows MESSENGER near Mercury's surface during its mission to study the planet.

Space Science

It is difficult to get a spacecraft into orbit around Mercury. For one thing, its nearness to the sun means that the sun's gravity is felt more strongly and disrupts a probe's orbit. Also, the changes in speed necessary to successfully enter orbit around the fast-moving planet would require a huge amount of rocket fuel.

A Lot Like the Moon

Images from Mariner 10 showed us that Mercury's surface looks a lot like the moon, covered with craters of various sizes as well as dark lava plains, mountains, and valleys. At one time in the distant past, Mercury was geologically active. This means that its surface was changing and shifting because of the effects of volcanoes and other geological processes. However, now there are no new lava flows to cover over the impact craters left when other objects crash into its surface.

Mapping Mercury

Mariner 10 mapped only about half of Mercury's surface, so it was not until the MESSENGER mission sent back data that we were able to see the rest of the planet in detail. These images showed that the planet's surface is even more jumbled than that of the moon. The largest crater, Caloris Basin, is about 960 miles (1,550 km) wide. The impact that created it was so huge that on the opposite side of the planet, it left an odd, hilly area, known as the "Weird Terrain."

This image shows Mercury's largest crater, the Caloris Basin. The area is also marked with a number of smaller craters.

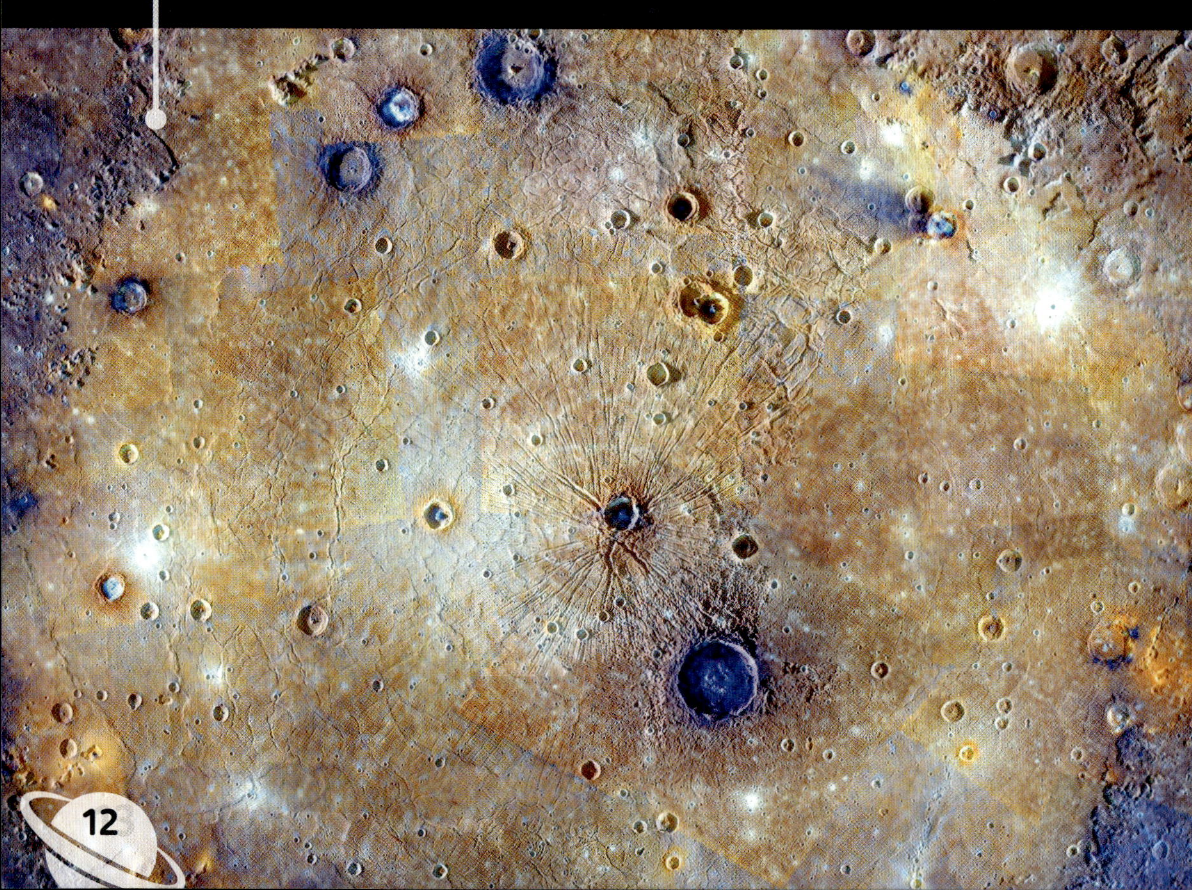

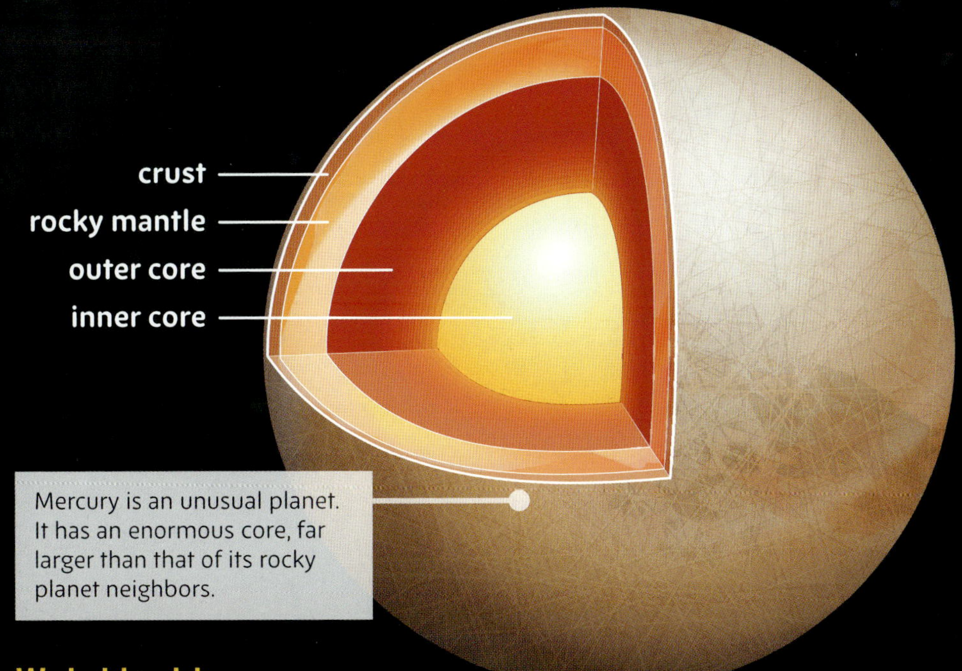

Mercury is an unusual planet. It has an enormous core, far larger than that of its rocky planet neighbors.

Weird Inside

Mercury is equally weird on the inside. Like the other rocky planets, it has a metal core, surrounded by a thick, slowly moving mantle of hot rock, with a rocky crust on the outside. However, its core must be huge, making up nearly half of its volume. Astronomers can infer this based on data about the planet's density and size. One theory is that Mercury was once much bigger, but a large object crashed into it, blasting away much of the mantle and crust while leaving the core intact. Another idea is that the heat of the young sun vaporized much of its surface rock. One of MESSENGER's goals was to learn more about the core.

SPACE SCIENCE

Some of Mercury's more unusual features are the folds (called rupes) that run across the plains. Astronomers believed that these rupes were formed when the planet's interior cooled, making the whole planet shrink. The crust had already solidified and was now too big for what was inside, so it wrinkled as the planet shrank.

Orbiting the Sun

Based on its movement across the sky, astronomers have known since ancient times that Mercury orbits the sun approximately once every 88 days. As it is so close, the sun's gravity exerts a huge force on the tiny planet, making it travel quickly: about 30 miles per second (48 kps). Mercury's path is elliptical (a little like a squished circle), and when it is at its closest point to the sun, it travels more quickly.

Every planet in our solar system makes a journey around the sun. This image shows the path some of the planets take.

A Locked Planet

It has proven to be much more difficult to learn how fast Mercury rotates on its axis. Until the 1960s, many astronomers believed that Mercury was "tidally locked." This would mean that it took the same amount of time to rotate on its axis as it did to complete one orbit of the sun, causing the same side of the planet always to face the sun. Earth's moon is tidally locked in this way, which is why we always see the same side from Earth.

Dark and Hot Mercury

However, radar astronomy in the 1960s showed that the dark side of Mercury was much hotter than would be expected. If it never faced the sun, that side should be incredibly cold, but this was not the case. From this data, scientists extrapolated a rotational period of about 59 days. This was a surprise to the scientific community, and some tried to think of other ways to account for the high temperatures. In the end, data from Mariner 10 confirmed the shorter rotation.

Astronomer Giuseppe Colombo (1920–1984) noted that for every two orbits of the sun, Mercury rotates three times on its axis.

Space History

In 1859, a French astronomer named Urbain Le Verrier (1811–1877) noticed anomalies in Mercury's orbit. He thought they were caused by the gravitational pull of another object orbiting closer to the sun. After all, Le Verrier had already used similar anomalies in Uranus's orbit to successfully predict the existence of Neptune. He named this hypothetical planet Vulcan, and for years, astronomers searched for it in the skies. Vulcan does not exist, but it was not until 1915 that Albert Einstein's theory of general relativity explained the irregularities in Mercury's orbit.

An artist's impression of Vulcan

Not Given Enough Attention

Compared to the other inner planets, Mercury has been largely neglected by astronomers. Even the James Webb and Hubble Space Telescopes do not study Mercury—pointing their delicate optics at something so close to the sun could damage them permanently. However, all that is changing with BepiColombo. The mission, named after Giuseppe Colombo, is a joint project of the European Space Agency (ESA) and the Japanese Aerospace Exploration Agency (JAXA).

Two Spacecrafts

BepiColombo is actually two separate spacecraft: the Mercury Planet Orbiter (MPO), which is built by ESA, and JAXA's Mercury Magnetospheric Orbiter (MMO). The MPO is focused on researching the surface and internal composition of the planet, while the MMO studies the planet's magnetosphere. They are traveling together until they reach Mercury in 2025 and then they will go their separate ways. The MPO will orbit closer to the planet than the MMO.

A Mega Mission

The mission has a lot of work to do; astronomers hope that it will solve a lot of unanswered questions about Mercury. MESSENGER has already sent back a huge amount of data about Mercury, and BepiColombo is designed to complement that. It has even more measuring equipment and will follow a different orbit pattern. The MPO will travel closer to the planet's surface and should be able to take better images of Mercury.

BepiColombo was carried into space on an Ariane 5 rocket on 20 October, 2018.

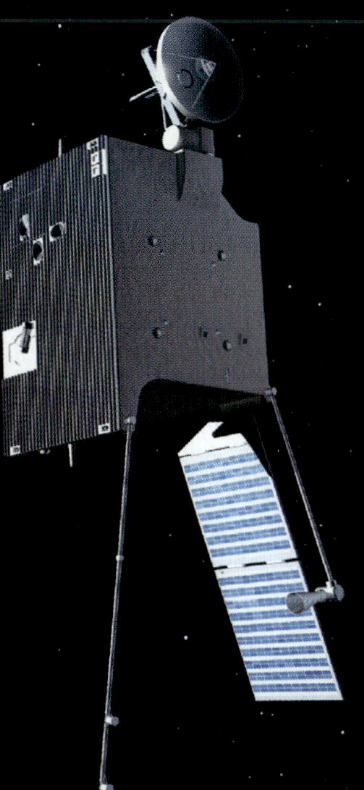

Space Science

The original plan for the BepiColombo mission included a small lander, the Mercury Surface Element. It would have been the first probe ever to land on the planet's surface, and was scheduled to operate for about a week. It would have carried cameras as well as tools for exploring Mercury's chemical composition and magnetic field, as well as a tiny rover. Unfortunately, this part of the mission was canceled in 2003 for budget reasons.

BepiColombo was charged with placing two orbiters around Mercury—MMO and MPO—to gather vital data about the planet.

A Burning Question

One question researchers want to answer is why Mercury's inner core is solid and why it is so large. They hope the MMO will return evidence of why such a small planet has a magnetic field, when even the larger Mars and Venus do not. The MPO will search for sulfur or water ice at the poles. Many of these discoveries will teach us more about the formation of the solar system.

Your Mission

You have been given the task of forming a global space agency. You must persuade other countries that such an agency could be more effective than single-country agencies. How would you encourage people to collaborate—what might motivate them to do so? Consider what a global agency could achieve that single-country agencies might not and the potential benefits to all countries.

Chapter 3

DISCOVERING VENUS

Venus is sometimes called Earth's twin, because of its similar size. However, telescopes, probes, and landers have shown that it is completely different—one of the last places in the solar system you would want to visit! In contrast to the beautiful bright object we see in the sky, closer observation has shown that Venus is a dangerous, inhospitable place.

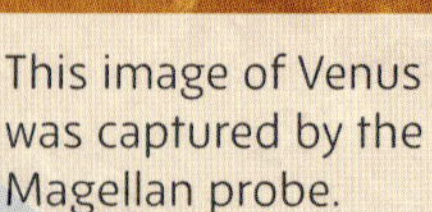

This image of Venus was captured by the Magellan probe.

Evidence of an Atmosphere

In 1761, a Russian astronomer, Mikhail Lomonosov (1711–1765), discovered evidence that Venus had an atmosphere. Venus has thick clouds, so it eluded close observation for centuries until astronomers started using other methods (such as radar mapping) in the 1950s and 1960s.

The First Probe to a Planet

In 1960, the Soviet spacecraft Venera 1 was launched. It was the first probe launched to another planet. However, it malfunctioned, and the National Aeronautics and Space Administration's (NASA's) Mariner 2 was the first to successfully fly past Venus, in 1962. It was followed by Mariner 5 and Mariner 10, which took images of Venus's clouds before traveling on to discover more about Mercury.

A Crash Landing

The Venera 3 probe crash-landed on Venus in 1966. It was the first spacecraft to reach the surface of another planet. In all, 10 Soviet probes managed to land on Venus's surface, but the space probes only managed to communicate with Earth for less than two hours. The high temperature and pressure on Venus completely destroyed probes within hours of landing.

A Space First

More data has been retrieved by spacecraft entering orbit around Venus. Venera 9 was the first spacecraft to enter orbit around Venus, in 1975. In addition to studying Venus's clouds and magnetosphere, it sent down a successful lander. Since then, several other probes have orbited Venus. In 1990, the NASA probe Magellan began its orbit around the planet. ESA's Venus Express mission entered orbit around Venus in 2006 and has sent back a huge amount of data. One key discovery is evidence that Venus may have had oceans in the past.

SPACE SCIENCE

Over the course of its four-year mission, Magellan was able to use radar mapping to "see" through the clouds on Venus. It provided incredibly accurate maps of 98 percent of the planet's surface.

The Magellan spacecraft begins its long journey to the planet Venus as part of its mapping mission.

The surface of Venus is a violent and volcanic place. Some of the volcanoes on the planet are far larger than those on Earth.

A Lot We Do Not Know

Despite the number of spacecraft that have visited Venus, there is still a lot we do not know about the planet. For example, scientists do not have enough data to be confident about Venus's internal structure. Venus's size and mass are so close to that of Earth that we assume it has a core, mantle, and crust, like Earth does. We do know that since the planet formed, Venus has been cooling at a similar rate to Earth, so its core is probably at least partially liquid, like Earth's is.

What We Have Learned

Thanks to the radar images provided by the Magellan spacecraft, we do know a lot about the surface of Venus. Most of it was shaped by volcanic activity, and measurements of sulfur in the atmosphere have led to theories that there might still be volcanic activity taking place on Venus. There are more than 150 volcanoes that are more than 60 miles (97 km) across. In 2023 scientists used radar images from Magellan to show that some of these volcanoes are active today.

Plains and Plains

Most of the planet's surface is covered by smooth volcanic plains. There are also two large masses of higher land, which are often called continents. Unlike continents on Earth, these are not surrounded by oceans, but in the distant past, they might have been. Ishtar Terra, in the north, is about the size of Australia. Aphrodite Terra, in the south, is bigger.

Surviving Erosion

Venus has far fewer craters than Mercury, and they have been eroded by wind or volcanic activity. None of them are smaller than 2 miles (3.2 km) across, because smaller objects would burn up while passing through Venus's thick atmosphere. Astronomers believe that volcanic activity has decreased dramatically since the last time the planet's surface was completely re-covered by lava.

Space Science

There is evidence that Venus had moving tectonic plates billions of years ago, but not today. This means that its crust is not constantly "recycled" like Earth's is. Scientists estimate that Venus's crust is much older: about 300 to 600 million years old, as opposed to Earth's, which is 100 million years old.

Except for Earth, Venus has by far the fewest impact craters of any rocky planet.

Hidden by Clouds

In the time between the discovery of Venus's atmosphere in 1761 and the first radar mapping of its surface in the 1960s, many people believed that its clouds hid a lush planet, similar to Earth, with rain forests or oceans covering the surface. However, modern observation techniques have shown us that Venus's atmosphere is anything but lush.

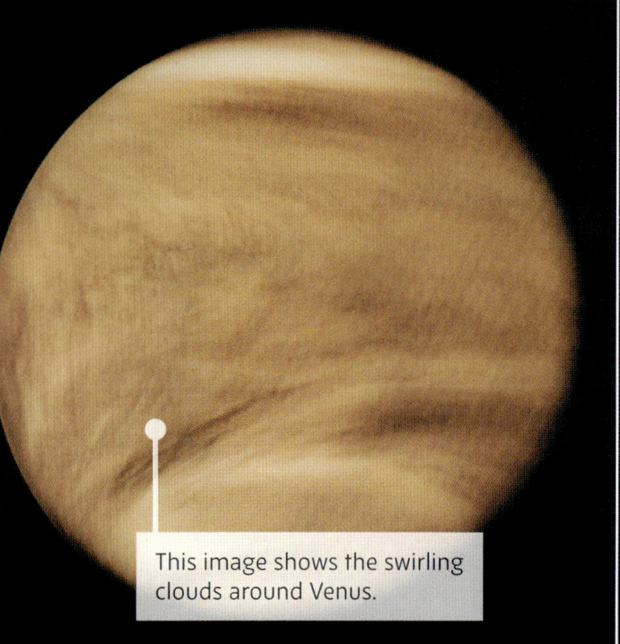

This image shows the swirling clouds around Venus.

Beneath the planet's clouds, Venus is extremely hot with a toxic atmosphere that makes life impossible.

Nothing Could Survive

In the late 1950s, microwave observations showed extremely high temperatures on Venus: more than 600 degrees Fahrenheit (316 °C). No forest or ocean could exist on a planet that hot! The thick, dense clouds, made up mainly of carbon dioxide, provide a vision of a greenhouse effect gone out of control. The clouds on Venus let in energy from the sun, then trap it there, with the result that Venus is the hottest planet in the solar system. It is hotter than Mercury, even though it is farther from the sun.

Life Might Be Possible

Other readings showed lower temperatures, and scientists were not sure if the high temperatures existed on the planet's surface or up in its atmosphere. It turns out that high in the atmosphere, the temperature is lower, a little more like Earth's. One interesting theory is the possibility that life—in the form of tiny microbes—may exist there. Long ago, when Venus still had oceans, they may have contained life. When the thick atmosphere caused the planet to heat up and the oceans to evaporate, these life forms could have adapted to instead live in the clouds. More research is needed to prove or disprove this theory.

Mission Impossible

In addition to high temperatures, Venus has extremely high atmospheric pressure: about 90 times that of Earth. These two factors make manned missions to the planet's surface impossible at least for now. Even landers do not survive for long there before being crushed by the atmosphere.

SPACE SCIENCE

Twice every 100 years or so, Venus transits the sun. The last pair of transits were in 2004 and 2012, and they were used by astronomers as an opportunity to study Venus's atmosphere. They were able to use spectroscopy to analyze sunlight passing through the planet's atmosphere and determine what chemicals it contained.

Venus

This image shows Venus's last transit of the sun, when it passed the star in 2012.

A Perfect Circle

We have discovered Venus's orbit time, but finding its rotation time has proven to be very difficult. Astronomers had used the surface features on Mercury (such as bright or dark plains) as landmarks to estimate how long it took to rotate. However, the clouds on Venus made that approach impossible. For example, the astronomer Jean-Dominique Cassini (1625–1712) lived before it was known that Venus had an atmosphere. He thought patterns in the clouds were surface features, and the astronomer estimated the rotation period as 24 hours.

Measuring the Rotation

Cassini's theory persisted for hundreds of years, and it was not until 1961 that radar was used to accurately measure Venus's rotation period at 243 Earth days. The planet takes about 225 Earth days to orbit the sun. That means a day on Venus is longer than a year on the planet! What was even more unusual was the discovery in 1964 that Venus's rotation is retrograde.

How Planets Move

Most planets rotate in the same direction as they orbit the sun. If you could look down at the solar system from above, you would see the planets moving counterclockwise around the sun at the same time as they rotate counterclockwise on their axes. However, although Venus travels counterclockwise around the sun like the rest of the planets, it rotates clockwise on its axis.

SPACE SCIENCE

The combination of Venus's long days, relatively short years, and retrograde rotation make for an unusual calendar. If you could stand on the surface of Venus, you would see the sun rise in the west and set in the east. It would take almost 117 days from sunrise to sunset, though!

Venus's path around the sun is a nearly perfect circle, and it completes one orbit about every 225 days.

It is hoped that missions such as Parker Solar Probe, shown here passing Venus, will tell us more about the fascinating planet.

A Lot to Learn

There is still a lot to learn about Venus. NASA's Parker Solar Probe has performed several flybys of Venus on its way to the sun, and BepiColombo conducted flybys in 2020 and 2021, although its main target is Mercury. Other missions have been planned and are awaiting approval, including one that would take samples of the surface and study the composition of the crust in more detail.

YOUR MISSION

Imagine you are in command of a mission to Venus to look for life. Consider:

- What key features you would search for (think about what you have learned about life on Earth and conditions necessary for it)
- What equipment you would use to explore the planet given its dangerous conditions

Chapter 4

DISCOVERING MARS

Without a doubt, after our home planet Earth, Mars is the best-explored planet in the solar system. Dozens of spacecraft have been launched to study the planet, and as a result, we know a lot about it. The first spacecraft to reach Mars showed that many previous ideas—including theories about oceans, plants, and life on the planet—were in fact wrong.

Since its launch in 2004, ESA's Mars Express probe has provided amazing pictures of Mars.

Failure Then Success

After a number of failed missions, NASA's Mariner 4 probe flew past Mars in 1965, taking the first close-up images of the surface of another planet. The information it sent back about Mars's surface, temperature, and atmospheric pressure led to a rethink of designs for landers. A Soviet lander mission was launched in 1971, and although its orbiter was successful, the lander crash-landed. A second lander, later in the same year, became the first to successfully land on the planet. The Viking 1 and Viking 2 probes, launched in 1975, were a huge success, and their landers sent back crucial information about the planet's surface, weather, and magnetosphere.

Space Science

The Soviet Mars 3 mission was the first lander to achieve a soft landing on Mars, rather than just crashing into the surface. The probe had taken more than six months to reach the planet, but it transmitted for only 14.5 seconds before the signal failed. It sent back just one partial image.

A New Age

The year 1997 marked the first successful Mars mission in two decades, when the Mars Pathfinder mission landed the wheeled robot Sojourner. It was followed in 2003 by the Mars Exploration Rover mission, which put Spirit and Opportunity on the surface of the planet. The much larger Curiosity rover landed in 2012. Its upgraded twin, Perseverance, landed in 2021.

Studying from the Skies

While rovers moved across the surface of Mars, a series of orbiters continued to study the planet from the skies. The Mars Global Surveyor mission then carried out detailed mapping between 1999 and 2006, followed by the Mars Odyssey and Mars Express missions. The MAVEN orbiter and the Mangalyaan orbiter reached Mars in 2014 to study the planet's atmosphere. Then in 2021, the Tianwen-1 orbiter, lander, and rover also arrived at Mars.

The Zhurong rover takes a group selfie with the Tianwen-1 lander!

Explored by Robots

Aside from the moon, Mars is the only planet in the solar system to have been explored by robotic rovers. These small-wheeled vehicles can send back information that would simply be impossible to obtain from an orbiting spacecraft. For example, rovers can dig into soil, drill into rocks, and carry out detailed chemical analysis. The way they move over the surface of a planet gives us far more data about what it is like.

What We Do Know

We now know that the surface of Mars is dry, dusty, and rocky. The surface is covered by a thin layer of iron oxide (commonly called rust), which gives it its red color. Giant sandstorms sometimes sweep across the planet, blocking the view of the orbiters circling it. Mars's surface does not have moving tectonic plates like Earth, so this has led to the formation of large volcanoes (now inactive) and also the deepest valley in the solar system. The tallest mountain in the solar system, the volcano Olympus Mons, is on Mars.

This illustration of a spacecraft after touchdown on Mars shows its solar panels fully deployed so the spacecraft can begin operations to collect samples.

The tallest peak in our solar system, Olympus Mons, is shown here, pictured by ESA's Mars Express probe.

Different Long Ago

It is certain that at one point, the surface of Mars was very different from today, with liquid water covering the planet in rivers and oceans. Now, the temperature and atmospheric pressure of the planet are both too low to allow liquid water to exist on the surface. However, there is ice there, which is easily visible in the form of ice caps at its poles.

Photographic Evidence

Early missions to Mars returned images showing what looked like dry riverbeds and canyons. More recent missions have sent back data confirming the presence of ice beneath the surface of the planet. In 2014, the Curiosity rover discovered that the soil where it is exploring contains about 2 percent water ice. This could be a huge help to any astronauts who visit Mars in the future, because carrying water with them from Earth is very expensive.

Space Science

Impact craters are common on Mars, because its extremely thin atmosphere offers it very little protection. Craters on Mars can last a long time, because there is no liquid water and little wind to erode them, and there are no active volcanoes to cover them with lava.

Journeying across the harsh and rocky terrain of Mars is a challenging task for any rover.

A Seventeenth-Century Study of Mars

In the seventeenth century, the German astronomer Johannes Kepler (1571–1630) studied the movement of Mars. At that point most people assumed that the planets followed perfectly circular paths around the sun (or around Earth, as some still believed). However, Mars's movement did not match up. Kepler used math to figure out that the planet must follow an elliptical path, with the sun not quite at the center. When Mars was closer to the sun, it traveled faster. Other planets also orbit like this, and the discovery helped Kepler formulate his laws of planetary motion.

Once Every 24 Hours

Mars rotates around its axis once every 24 hours, 39 minutes, and 35 seconds, making the length of a day on Mars almost identical to a day on Earth. However, the Martian year is nearly twice as long at 687 Earth days. Mars's axis also tilts at a similar angle to Earth, giving it seasons. However, because of Mars's irregular path, the seasons are not the same length—for example, spring lasts for seven months, and winter for just four. Even in the summer, it is not hot: it might reach 65 degrees Fahrenheit (18 °C) during the day and drop to -130 degrees Fahrenheit (-90 °C) at night.

Not Alone

Unlike Mercury and Venus, Mars is not alone in its patch of the solar system. It is orbited by two small moons, Deimos and Phobos. Compared to Earth's moon, they really are tiny: Deimos is fewer than 8 miles (13 km) across, and Phobos is about 14 miles (22.5 km) in diameter. They are lumpy and irregularly shaped, and they orbit very close to the planet. In 1971, when Mariner 9 visited Mars and found it covered by a dust storm, it studied and took images of Phobos while waiting for the dust on Mars to clear.

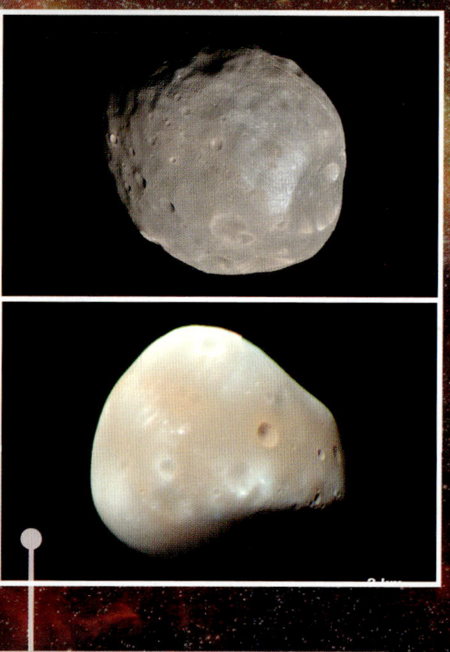

Phobos is shown top here, with Deimos below. Both are small and lumpy with many craters.

SPACE SCIENCE

The Martian atmosphere is so thin that it is hardly there at all: it is about 1 percent of Earth's atmosphere. It is mainly made up of carbon dioxide, but it is too thin to trap the sun's heat and cause a greenhouse effect. As a result, temperatures can drop to -225 degrees Fahrenheit (-143 °C) at the poles during winter.

Mars is gold, brown, and tan in color, which contributes to its reddish appearance. The colors are due to the rusting of iron, which is present in the dusty surface of the Red Planet.

Could Life Be There?

Ever since Giovanni Schiaparelli's drawing of "canals" on Mars, people have been fascinated by the idea that life exists there. Although we know that the Martians of science-fiction books and movies do not exist, the possibility remains that simple life in some form existed on Mars in the past and may still exist today. After all, there was once abundant liquid water on the planet, and there is still ice. Any life on Mars would have to be different from most life on Earth. For example, there is no oxygen in the Martian atmosphere, and the temperature is extremely low.

Testing for Life

The Viking landers in the 1970s carried out simple tests to see if there were microbes in the soil. They took a sample of soil and exposed it to chemicals that would feed any microbial life living there. Some gases were produced, which could have been the result of microbes' life processes. However, most scientists now think the results can be explained by more simple chemical processes.

Space Science

No Mars mission has ever brought back soil samples to Earth, but scientists have found nearly 300 meteorites on Earth that we know came from Mars. Three of these show possible evidence of ancient life: tiny structures that resemble fossilized bacteria. There is no definitive proof of life either way, but scientists continue to analyze these amazing rocks.

This artist's image shows how Mars may have looked long ago, when water was present on the planet's now-dry surface.

One Main Goal

The Phoenix lander explored Mars in 2008 with the goal of finding a zone within the planet's soil where microbial life could exist. Although the lander could not drive around, it had a robotic arm that allowed it to dig trenches. It discovered that Mars's soil contains a toxic chemical called perchlorate, which is harmful to life. Several years later, the Curiosity rover found even more perchlorate.

Finding Signs

However, Curiosity also found several positive signs. It explored the remains of a former freshwater lake and found chemicals that form naturally in drinkable water, where life could form. It has also detected key elements such as carbon, hydrogen, nitrogen, and phosphorus. More recently, its mission has changed to focus on the search for evidence of ancient past life, including organic molecules and fossils.

Curiosity is traveling across the surface of Mars, searching for signs of life on its rocky home.

YOUR MISSION

If you were in command of a mission to Mars to collect soil samples, what factors would you need to consider? Bear in mind:

- Potential hazards and how you could deal with them
- How you could safeguard crewmembers and people on Earth from any contamination
- Equipment you might need

Chapter 5

FIGURING OUT SPACE

The invention of the telescope in the early 1600s revolutionized astronomy, leading to amazing new discoveries about the solar system. However, since the Space Age began in the late 1950s, our knowledge about the planets themselves has increased at an even greater rate. In addition to sending astronauts to the moon, unmanned probes have mapped the craters of Mercury, peered through the clouds of Venus, and rolled across the rocky surface of Mars.

Big Questions

Some people question why we spend so much time, effort, and money studying other planets. After all, they say, there are serious problems—such as climate change and disease—on Earth. Should we not focus on solving our own problems before worrying about the ancient history of Venus? That is an important question to ask.

Astronaut Edwin Aldrin is captured here standing on the surface of the moon in 1969, during the historic moon landing.

The International Space Station (ISS) is one of the most famous crewed projects in space, with many international astronauts participating in studies on board the Station.

Getting to Know Your Neighbors

Dr John Spencer, a scientist who worked on the Cassini mission that studied Saturn, once said, "Well, you know, you can spend your life in your house, or you can get out and get to know your neighborhood." This is what NASA, ESA, and other space agencies are doing—by studying Earth's near neighbors in space, we are gaining important insights into how Earth and the rest of the solar system formed.

We Have to Learn

We cannot discover how planets form and change by studying only Earth. The world we know is the result of complex forces that have operated for billions of years. Things might have worked out very differently if Earth was closer to the sun, had a thinner atmosphere, or had an axis tilted at a different angle. Studying other planets also gives us insight into the future. For example, conditions on Venus and Mars offer clues about what Earth might be like billions of years in the future.

SPACE HISTORY

At the beginning of the Space Age, the United States and Soviet Union went head-to-head, each trying to outdo the other and be the first to reach key milestones. Since then, other countries have played their part. ESA joined the field in the mid-1970s, and in recent years Japan, China, and India have become major players. The Indian Space Research Organisation (ISRO) sent a mission that entered Mars's orbit in 2014 and studied the planet for eight years before contact was lost.

Living on Another Planet

One question that space exploration has tried to answer is whether humans could live on other planets, either permanently or temporarily. After all, astronauts live on the ISS for months at a time. One day, it may become necessary for humans to colonize other worlds to survive. Another reason for setting up colonies on other worlds would be to make use of their resources, by mining valuable substances and sending them back to Earth.

Like Living on Earth

Living on another planet would mean recreating conditions similar to those on Earth. Human colonists would need air to breathe, water to drink, and food to eat. They would need to be protected from extreme temperatures and solar radiation. They would also need to find out how to remain fit and healthy in places with lower gravity and atmospheric pressure.

The ISS (right) has everything that humans need to survive. A colony on a planet or other space body would need to be equally well equipped.

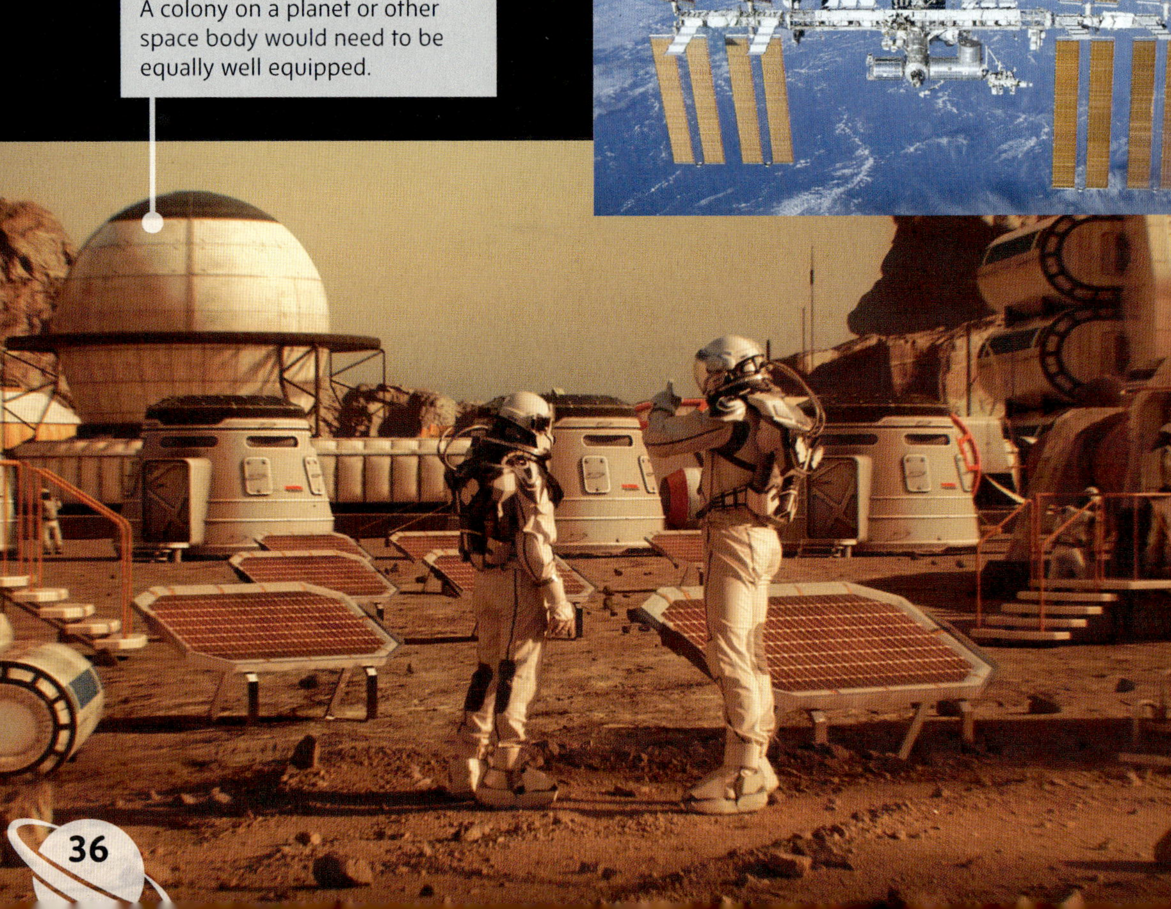

Growing food crops on Mars would be essential for a colony of humans to survive there in the long term.

Difficult Challenges

Mercury's position near the sun would make colonization difficult; any settlement would have to be near the poles. However, Mercury does have a magnetic field, which could help protect colonists from cosmic rays and solar storms. Its gravity is less than Earth's but still about twice that of the moon. Mars is the most likely candidate, but it would still be incredibly difficult. It has frozen water, but it is very cold and has little atmosphere and no magnetosphere to protect colonists from the dangers of radiation.

SPACE SCIENCE

It would be virtually impossible to set up a colony on the surface of Venus, where the temperature is hot enough to melt lead. About 30 miles (48 km) above the surface, however, the atmosphere provides a potential habitat. The atmospheric pressure and temperature are similar to Earth's, and scientists have proposed floating settlements held up by balloons.

A Manned Mission

The first step toward setting up a colony would be to send a manned mission to explore the planet and then return. However, even that presents significant challenges. For example, a trip to Mars would take at least six months, and with current technology it would be impossibly expensive to send the huge amount of water, food, and other supplies astronauts would need.

A Huge Leap

Some scientists have taken the idea of colonization a step farther and explored the possibility of "terraforming" other planets. This literally means "Earth-shaping," and it involves deliberately changing a body to be more like Earth. The idea may sound like science fiction, and that is one of the origins of the concept. However, we have already seen that human actions play a role in the weather and other conditions on Earth. Is it really such a huge leap to think that we could change conditions on other planets, too?

This image shows Mars in key stages of terraforming, from the planet as it is today, far left, to an Earthlike home, far right.

Mainly Mars

Mars is one of the main candidates for terraforming. Its thin atmosphere is mainly carbon dioxide, which is a greenhouse gas, so if we could thicken the atmosphere, it would help heat the planet. Heating the planet would release more carbon dioxide, currently frozen at the poles, and accelerate the heating process. However, Mars's lack of a magnetic field like Earth's is a significant problem, and at the moment, the technology to provide a planetary-scale magnetic field does not exist.

A Lot of Change

Terraforming Venus would require reducing the surface temperature and changing the atmosphere by getting rid of most of the carbon dioxide and sulfur dioxide and replacing it with nitrogen and oxygen. Venus receives about twice as much sunlight as Earth, so one possible way of reducing

This artist's impression shows astronauts on the surface of Mars outside a domelike building with a vehicle for transporation.

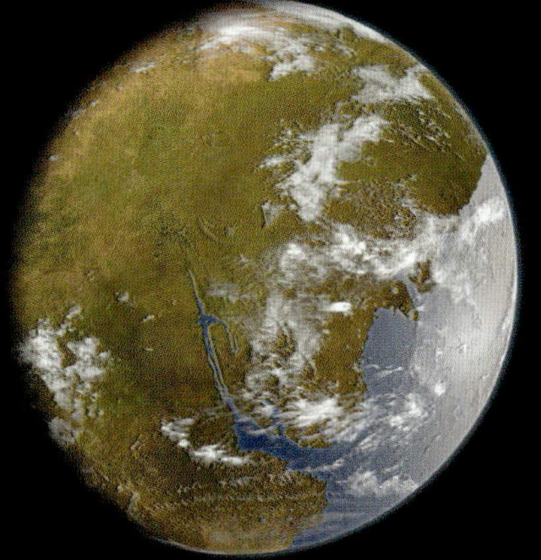

the temperature would be to put up a large solar shade. Another idea is to introduce bacteria into the atmosphere, which would take carbon from the atmosphere.

Just an Idea

At the moment, terraforming is just a concept. Scientists have not yet developed all the technologies that would be needed, and no missions are planned. In addition, many people question the ethics of terraforming and wonder if humans have the right to alter other planets.

Space Science

In his 1898 novel *The War of the Worlds*, the author H.G. Wells (1866–1946) tells the story of a Martian invasion of Earth. The Martians bring a type of red weed from Mars, which grows so quickly that it engulfs the native Earth plants. This is a kind of reverse terraforming, in which Earth is transformed to be more suitable for alien species.

YOUR MISSION

If you were in command of a mission to terraform another planet, how would you plan the task? Consider:

- The key features that are essential for life—what are they and how would you create them?
- The nonessential features that are not required for life, but that humans value because they enhance their quality of life
- The STEM skills you and your team members would need to successfully complete the mission

Chapter 6

ALWAYS MORE MISSIONS

No matter how much we discover about other planets, there is always much more to learn. Space missions take years to plan and prepare, so while one probe is in orbit around a distant planet, the next two or three are already in the pipeline. For example, Venus has been visited by BepiColombo (on its way to Mercury) and Parker Solar Probe (on its way to study the sun). Missions farther into the future, such as Russia's Venera-D, designed to map future landing sites, are already in the planning stages. Engineers are working on a way to design a lander that can last for more than a few hours in Venus's harsh and violent conditions.

BepiColombo has provided us with many fascinating facts about planets such as Venus and Mercury, shown in the image above.

Focus on Mars

At the moment, though, most attention is focused on Mars. There are multiple rovers and landers on the surface, with several probes in orbit around the planet, and there are many more planned. One proposed mission will set up a network of meteorological stations to provide a clearer picture of the planet's weather. Still others will try to return samples of Martian soil and rock to Earth.

Headline-Grabbing Missions

The missions that get all the headlines, though, are manned missions to Mars. Several space agencies have proposed sending astronauts to Mars before 2040. Some plans involve sending colonists on a one-way trip, but there are many technological hurdles to clear before such a mission could succeed.

Space Science

Humans are not really designed for long space flights. We need a lot of food and water, we produce waste that must be disposed of, and we have a habit of getting sick or injured. Some people have proposed sending more robots instead of humans to Mars. After all, a robot does not need to be fed, and it will not get bored during the years of travel. There is already a robot working on the ISS. Could the next step be to send a robotic astronaut to explore Mars?

Robots could lead the way in space investigation, and also assist humans when they make manned missions to space bodies.

Not Easy Missions

Future missions to other planets face significant challenges—for one thing, the distances involved are huge. It takes most spacecraft between 6 and 12 months to reach Mars. That is fine for a robot but difficult for a living, breathing human. Using more fuel could make the trip go faster, but that would mean taking a huge load of fuel, which brings us to the second problem: weight. Launching anything into space is expensive; currently it costs about $10,000 for every pound you want to launch into space. A rocket capable of carrying several people to Mars will not be light!

Blue-Sky Thinking

Space engineers are having to think outside the box to come up with ways to solve these problems. New technologies may allow spacecraft to go faster and farther and to do it more cheaply. One innovation, the ion drive, has already been put to the test and was used on the Dawn probe, which was a mission that studied asteroids. Another idea, using a solar sail, requires no fuel at all. Instead, it relies on the force of the "solar wind"—the pressure of radiation from the sun.

Space Science

An ion drive works by bombarding a gas—usually xenon—with electrons. This turns the atoms of gas into positively charged ions, which move around at high speeds. When the ions reach a high enough speed, they are focused into an ion beam that shoots out the back and thrusts the spacecraft forward. The amount of fuel needed is small compared to a conventional rocket engine, and ion drives can achieve much higher speeds but at much lower acceleration.

The Japanese IKAROS space probe captures energy from the sun to power it as it travels through space.

It is possible that with our advancing technology we will even be able to create generation ships that can carry many people through space for years—perhaps searching for other planets to call home.

Hard at Work

Scientists are hard at work on other technologies to enable astronauts to travel to other planets. In addition to new methods of powering spacecraft, engineers must develop more efficient ways of recycling water and air and providing food, as well as methods of protecting them from the high levels of radiation they will encounter.

YOUR MISSION

You have been given the mission of designing a spacecraft that can travel to another planet such as Mars. When creating your design, consider:

- Living accommodation needed for the crew
- Food and drink required, and how and where to store it
- The social, physical, and mental wellbeing of the crew

FUTURE MISSIONS

NASA sent 12 astronauts to the surface of the moon in the 1960s and '70s, but since then, no human has traveled more than a few hundred miles above Earth's surface. Space travel is both expensive and dangerous, and once astronauts reached the moon, the focus shifted to unmanned probes. We have learned a great amount from the spacecraft that have visited other planets, but can it compare with the thrill of seeing an astronaut broadcast live from the surface of Mars?

Private Missions

Until recently, it was only the governments of large countries that were able to launch space missions. However, in the past decade, more private companies are getting involved. Some are already making money by taking tourists into space, while others are focused on goals such as sending astronauts to Mars. Much of this is driven by economics. NASA, for example, has allowed private companies to take over the delivery of cargo and crew to the ISS. More competition could mean better prices.

It is likely that Mars will be the first planet that we attempt to colonize. Who knows where our missions will take us next?

Big Investment, New Technology

Several lucrative prizes have sparked interest in space flight and led to huge investment in new technologies. The Ansari X Prize offered $10 million to the first commercial organization to launch a reusable manned spacecraft into space twice within two weeks. The Google Lunar XPrize offered a $30 million prize for privately funded missions to land a robot on the moon.

All Teamwork

Whether it is a government agency or a private company that sends the first astronaut to another planet, it will take a huge team to get them there. More research into all aspects of space technology is needed, and some of those technologies may prove useful on Earth as well.

YOUR FUTURE MISSION

Perhaps this book has inspired you to find out more about the inner planets. Maybe, one day, you'll even carve out a career in space science and make it your mission to explore the mysteries of the universe and unlock its secrets.

GLOSSARY

astronomers scientists who study planets, stars, and other objects beyond Earth

atmosphere the layer of gases surrounding a planet

atmospheric pressure the pushing force of the weight of the gases in the atmosphere

axis an imaginary line through the center of a planet, around which it rotates

craters hollow areas, like the inside of a bowl, created when an object crashes into a planet or other large object

flyby a flight past an object to make observations. When a spacecraft does a flyby of a planet, it does not stop or enter orbit

galaxy hundreds of billions of stars and other matter held together by gravity

gravity the force that pulls all objects toward each other

lander a spacecraft designed to land on the surface of a planet or other object and send back data

light-years units of distance equal to the distance light can travel in one year–about 6 trillion miles (9.46 trillion km)

magnetic field the space around a magnet in which a magnetic force is active

magnetosphere the region surrounding a planet or other object in which its magnetic field is the dominant magnetic field

meteorites lumps of stone or metal from meteors that have landed on Earth

microbes tiny living things that can be seen only with a microscope. Bacteria are a type of microbe

microwave a type of high-frequency radio wave. It can be used to send information over long distances

orbit the curved path that one body in space takes around another, such as a moon orbiting a planet

poles the ends of a planet's axis

probe an instrument or tool used to explore something that cannot be observed directly

radar the use of radio waves to track the location, distance, and speed of faraway objects. Waves are sent out and then picked up again when they bounce back after hitting an object

radiation waves of energy sent out by sources of heat or light, such as the sun. Radiation can be harmful to living things

retrograde moving in the opposite direction. Venus has a retrograde rotation on its axis: clockwise as opposed to the other planets' counterclockwise

rover a robotic vehicle that is capable of driving across the surface of a planet, moon, or other object in space

solar system the sun and everything in orbit around it, such as planets, asteroids, and comets

tectonic plates the segments of Earth's crust that move around in relation to one another. The movement of tectonic plates causes earthquakes and volcanoes

terraforming causing changes to another object in space that will make it more like Earth

transit when a planet or other object passes directly between Earth and the sun, so that it can be seen from Earth as it moves across the disc of the sun

BOOKS

Baby Professor. *Inner Vs Outer Planets! How Are Planets Different in Our Solar System?* Baby Professor, 2024.

Barr, Catherine. *Voyage Through the Solar System* (Space Voyage). Rosen Publishing Group, 2022.

Hawking, Stephen and Lucy Hawking. *Unlocking the Universe: Everything You Need to Travel Through Space and Time*. Puffin Books, 2021.

WEBSITES

Find out more about astronomy at:
kids.britannica.com/students/article/astronomy/272989

Discover more about our solar system at:
kids.britannica.com/students/article/solar-system/277129

Learn more about our solar system and the inner planets at:
https://science.nasa.gov/learn/basics-of-space-flight/chapter1-2

Publisher's note to educators and parents:
All the websites featured above have been carefully reviewed to ensure that they are suitable for students. However, many websites change often, and we cannot guarantee that a site's future contents will continue to meet our high standards of educational value. Please be advised that students should be closely monitored whenever they access the Internet.

INDEX

ABOUT THE AUTHOR

Sarah Eason has written many children's books and has a particular interest in space science. She has found researching and writing this book fascinating and hopes that it helps readers better understand the mysteries of space and maybe make it their mission to become a future space explorer.